MARGARET SILF

Sacred
IN
THE
City

For Ruth and for Isobel, in love and gratitude for lifelong friendships, forged between the steel mills and the Pennine peaks of our native city, Sheffield

Contents

PROLOGUE: *At the City Gates*

A traveller arrived one day at the gates of a city. He asked the watchman, "What's the name of this city, and what are the people like here?" The watchman replied: "Where are you from?" The traveller named his own home town. "And what are the people like in your home town?" "Well," said the traveller, "they are not very friendly. They are rude and selfish and unwelcoming." "In that case," said the watchman, "I think you will find people here are very much like they are where you live." So the traveller went on his way, not wanting to stay in that town.

A second traveller arrived at the gate and asked the watchman. "What town is this, and what are the people like here?" And again the watchman asked, "Where are you from?" The visitor named the same town as the first traveller. The watchman asked, "What are the people like where you come from?" The traveller replied: "They are very kind, always willing to help and ready with a friendly word for a stranger." The watchman smiled back and said, "I think you will find people here are very much like the folk in your own home town." And the traveller went into the city and stayed there.

Same city, different eyes. Perhaps what is true in the story is true in our own home town. The way we see it will determine what it means to us. If we see it as unfriendly and drab, it will become so. If we see it in a positive light, it could be a very different picture. Wherever we find ourselves, life is like a hall of mirrors; it tends to reflect back to us the expression and the attitude we bring to it.

How do we really see our home town? Perhaps familiarity has dulled our vision to a jaded view of the oft-trodden streets. But what if we could see afresh the divine light shining through the cracks in the dusty pavements, and hear the eternal song through the throb of the traffic noise?

This book invites you to look with new vision at your home town. This is the holy city – your city – alive with the sacred mystery all around you and deep within you.

Explore it with open eyes and an awakened heart, and enjoy all it has to show you.

"The treasure we look for is hidden in the ground on which we stand."
Henri J. M. Nouwen

"Where we love is home — home that our feet may leave, but not our hearts."

Oliver Wendell Holmes

AT HOME

This is your home town. But what does "home" mean to you? Is it just the place where you live, the address registered with the authorities? Or is your heart most truly at home with those you love, who may be very far from where you live? Or is "home" perhaps an inner sense of a state you cannot describe, the kind of indefinable "God-shaped space" in your heart that nothing on earth can completely fill?

I have an ornamental egg-shell on my desk, with a painted snail on it, inscribed with the words: "Home is where you go when you run out of places." It reminds me daily that wherever in the world I roam, there is always something beyond all the "places", however fascinating and inspiring those places may be. I have many "places" in my memory bank, but at the end of every journey, I return to a place I call my own. It's there that my roots go deep, anchored in long-standing friendships, a caring local community and a familiar landscape. Yet even here a large part of my

heart lives with those I love who are far away, and still strains after "I know not what", to fill the space that nothing on earth can ultimately satisfy.

But for most of us there will be one particular place that is home, however incomplete and unsatisfactory it may feel. It may be in the middle of a housing estate, or it may bask in its own grounds and garden. Whatever its location or market value, it is home. Spend a little while today getting in touch with that fact. This is your space. Can it also be your "sacred space"?

WHEN JESUS CAME TO CALL

Here is a story about a man, long ago, who had a surprise visitor to the place he called home.

Two thousand years ago a man you might not immediately choose as a friend was out and about in his home town of Jericho. His name was Zacchaeus, and he was a tax collector, a man of considerable wealth, not entirely honestly acquired.

Otherwise all we know about him is that he was short. Jesus was also passing through Jericho that day. Zacchaeus, eager to get a look at Jesus, climbed a tree to get a better view. Perhaps he wanted to see without being seen. Faith can easily become a spectator activity

– attendance without commitment. But Zacchaeus was in for a surprise. Far from remaining safely concealed among the leaves, he was to become the focus of Jesus' special attention. "Come down, Zacchaeus," said Jesus. "I'm coming home with you."

(Adapted from Luke 19:1–10)

Imagine if it had been you up there in the tree. How would you react if Jesus said, "Come on down. I'm coming home with you today"? Leaving aside the state of the bathroom, and the unwashed dishes, do these words fill you with joy or with dread? Zacchaeus, we hear, "welcomed him joyfully" (Luke 19:6), but the story doesn't quite end there…

Once back home, with his unexpected, uninvited guest, Zacchaeus has a transforming experience. The very presence of Jesus in his home opens his eyes and he begins to see himself as others see him. He admits to himself that he has been leading a dishonest life. He resolves to make fourfold restitution to anyone he has defrauded and give half of his personal wealth to the poor.

What a difference a day makes! Can you imagine you and Jesus having such a conversation? Without anything being said explicitly, you might feel someone was looking into your heart. Would that encourage you to make any changes at all? Can you also imagine Jesus' joy at being invited to be right there with you, in your home? Your home is an outward expression of who you are. A sacred presence has revealed itself right in the heart of your life. Can you connect more consciously to this sacredness, both when you are alone and when you are with others, knowing that when you have friends in for coffee or a meal, that sacred presence is also there among you, always there within and around you?

A favourite landmark of mine is an insignificant looking house on a busy main road not far from where I live. The ground floor is a shop. Above the shop is the family apartment. Right at the top is a little attic window, and just above that window are the initials of the person who, I assume, originally built the place. I can never pass that little house without reflecting on those three layers it contains, and seeing in them a reflection of my own life. There is a large part of my life that is like the shop – pursuing my own trade, as it were, doing the things I do, open to the wider world around me. Then there is a more private layer, where I relate to my family and friends and spend my leisure time. And up in the attic is a much smaller space that is shared only with God and, possibly, with a few trusted "soul-friends". Maybe I don't go there very often, or maybe I spend time there every day, in that sacred space, that inner sanctum where I consciously engage with the holy. That three-storey house is a parable of myself and my relationship with the world, with those I love, and with God.

AT HOME – WITH YOURSELF AND WITH GOD

- Take time to be still in your own home and reflect on what this "home" really means to you. Are you mainly contented or troubled in your own four walls? Who shares your home? Does it feel crowded, teeming with too many demands, or lonely after the children have left or following divorce or bereavement? Jesus once said, "*Make your home in me, as I make mine in you*" (John 15:4). Just let these words sink into your heart. Keep chewing them over when you have a few quiet moments. Note that there is no mention of "tidy up first and get yourself sorted, and then I might come". It is a simple, heartfelt promise that the holy one already resides with you, and always will, wherever your home is, and however you may feel about it. Let this promise take root in your heart, and grow stronger, day by day.

- Try thinking of yourself and your life in terms of the "three-storey house". What is your "shop" about? In what ways does your life relate to the wider world? What about your "opening hours"? Are public demands on your time and energy light, or excessive? How are things in your family space? How at ease are you in visiting the "attic", that inner space in your heart where you consciously meet with God? How do you feel about the *balance* between your public life, your private life and your inner life with God?

- The initials under the eaves say something about ownership. Are you truly at home in the place where you live? Can you drop your city masks when you close your front door, and be the person you feel you truly are? Are you truly at home in God and God in you? If this is your desire, can you let the desire flow into prayer?

- Can you find a corner of your home that could be your special space, perhaps for prayer or quiet time, or simply a space just to be reflective and still? Try marking it with some symbol, like a candle, a flower, a photo or some memento that means something to you. It can be simple and unobtrusive but it will provide a symbolic gateway into the presence of holiness all around you.
I have a friend who lives with a demanding family in an inner-city apartment. Her special space is just the view of a particular tree from her apartment window. It helps her to focus on the beauty and holiness beyond her, and then rediscover it, day by day, within her and around her.

"*The place God calls you to is the place where your deep gladness and the world's deep hunger meet.*"

Frederick Buechner

AT WORK

For some of us our home is also our place of work. But for most people, going to work involves leaving the comforts of home and venturing out to the office, classroom, hospital ward, workshop, factory or building site. Whereas "home" is a place to *be*, the workplace is where we are expected to *do*. It has sometimes been pointed out that we are human *beings*, not human *doings,* because the constant requirement to be *doing* can stifle our deeper need simply to *be*. Even so, we have to work to live, whether that work involves running a household and caring for a family, or working outside the home. Unless we contribute our own gifts and energies to the tasks of life, those tasks will not get done, and life as we know it will not continue.

Where do you work? In the home or outside it? What is your workplace like? It may seem unlikely that we would find traces of holiness in our workplace, but let's take a closer look. For this we need to look inside the factory walls, through the office windows and certainly beyond the pay cheque.

LIVING OUR PASSION

I once met a young man who had trained for a learned profession, but in the course of his long training he had discovered that this was not actually his true vocation. He told his parents he wanted to leave university and train, instead, as a cook. His parents then remembered that even as a small boy he had never tired of helping in the kitchen. They supported him in his plans, and he became an apprentice cook in a local restaurant and eventually a renowned chef in a leading hotel. The change was astounding. He came alive. He began to love his work. The passion was palpable. Regrettably most of us don't discover our passion until we think we are almost too old to follow it, but when you meet someone who is living out the best gifts within them, it really shows – and remember, it is never too late to fulfil the person you were created to be. We glimpse the sacredness of the workplace, whether in the home or outside of it, in the

people who are there, and in their passion and commitment to what they are doing.

In the Middle Ages a pilgrim once came upon a band of workers hewing away at blocks of stone. He asked one: "What are you doing?" The worker sighed and groaned as he reluctantly replied: "I'm trying to earn enough money to live on." He asked a second worker: "What are you doing?" The worker smiled contentedly as he answered: "I'm working so that I can care for my family and give them a better life." And then he asked a third worker: "What are you doing?" The worker raised his eyes to the skies, and replied with deep pride: "I'm building a cathedral." All three men were doing the same job. The difference lay in their attitude and motivation.

As you go about your normal work today, if someone were to ask you "What are you doing?" how would you respond?

SPENDING OUR GIFTS

As we work we use our gifts, our talents, and our experience. This is certainly for our own benefit, but it is also for the greater good, because what we do and how we do it affects all creation in some way. Let's visit an employer from biblical times as he challenges his employees to use their gifts.

There were once three people who worked for a shrewd businessman. One day he called them into his office. "I have to go away for a while," he told them. "While I'm gone I hope you will do your best to keep our business in good shape, and even expand it." With this, he gave the first employee £1,000, with the instruction to use it wisely so that it would be worth more on the employer's return. Then he gave the second employee £100, with the same instruction. And to the third he gave £10, with the same instruction.

The first employee, an engineer, thought hard about how to use his £1,000 and what he was best able to do, then purchased raw materials and applied himself to making a new product to bring to market. The second, a keen gardener, used the money to buy seeds and plants, and started a small market garden. In due course he brought his vegetables to the farmers' market and made a profit. But the third employee, a bit sulky because he had not been given much, thought to himself, "My employer is mean-spirited and he will be very angry if I risk his money." So he put the £10 in a box and hid it under the bed.

On his return the employer called them in again. "So what did you do with the money I gave you?" he asked. The first showed him the new product he had designed and gave him back £2,000 he had raised by selling it. The second brought him a sample of the fresh vegetables and gave him back the £200 he had raised at the farmers' market. But the third came back with the £10 he had been given. The employer was delighted to find that the first two employees had used the resources he had given them wisely, but he was disappointed with the third employee. "Why didn't you at least put the money in the bank," he asked, "where it would have gained a bit of interest?" "I was afraid of losing it," the man replied. "Now you have back what you gave me, no more, no less."

(Adapted from Matthew 25:14–30)

This story takes us to the heart of our own lives. What gifts have we been given? How are we using them? Gifts are for spending, not saving. Our lives are for spending, not saving. In the biblical story, the man who put his talents under the bed has them taken away from him, and given to someone else who will use them better. It sounds harsh, but it is nevertheless true that what we don't use will eventually become useless. Our gifts will get rusty. Our resources will lose their value. The warning "use it or lose it" could well be the title of this cautionary tale from long ago, as well as for our lives today.

WORKPLACE REFLECTIONS

- How would you describe your work – whether it is paid or unpaid, at home or outside the home? Reflect on those you work with, and take time to notice the divine within them. Where and how do you see God in your colleagues? What particular gifts do you see in them? And in yourself?

- What is your personal passion in life? How are you following it? We don't just discover and follow our passion in the workplace. You may be living your passion in ways that you don't regard as work, simply because you love doing them – for example, gardening, singing, baking, or DIY. If you can follow your dream and also be paid for it, you are very fortunate. But, paid or unpaid, when we are living our passion we are spending our gifts. We are using what we have been given in order to enrich all creation, and we are living true to our deepest calling.

- How do you feel about the balance in your life between *doing* and *being*? Do you feel uncomfortable in taking time out simply to relax? Or do you perhaps feel under-employed and even lethargic? Our lives are a bit like an oil lamp. The wick of the lamp has two ends. One end must remain submerged in the oil of a quiet reflective heart, while the other must be extended into the world of your daily life. Unless both these conditions are in place, there will be no flame. Take time to *be*, and you will have the energy to *do*.

"*The road behind us becomes what freed us for the road ahead.*"

Joan Chittister

ON THE MOVE

When you go to bed tonight you will not be the same person you were when you woke up this morning. You will have been affected and changed, whether slightly or significantly, by everyone you meet, every conversation you engage in, every choice you make. In the course of one day you will have made a unique journey. Magnify this thought into a lifetime, and you will see what change and transformation has been happening in you through the years. Life is never tidy. Life is a journey, in which the only predictable factor is unpredictability. It is an adventure that is constantly on the move. We have to run faster and faster to keep up with its pace. We feel its pressure whenever we board a train, travel on a bus, struggle with the commuter traffic or weave our way through the airport. How can we find God in all this flux? Is it possible to touch, and be touched by, the unchangeable, when we are all the time striving to find our footing in a constantly shifting world?

TRAVEL FRUSTRATIONS

Waiting for the bus, negotiating traffic congestion, sitting helplessly when the train grinds to an inexplicable halt: all these situations remind us that our journey is held in hands other than our own. Such conditions try our patience and tense our nerves. They can easily cause us to focus on life's irritations rather than its rewards, but they can be a necessary reminder that the world does not revolve solely around our personal needs and convenience.

Being on the move demands patience. Trains frequently slow to a crawl or stop dead for no apparent reason. Buses fail to arrive. Explanations for timetable irregularities can make us laugh or cry, depending on our mood. Such tribulations can also bond us more closely with our fellow travellers, and they are usually more trivial in hindsight than they appear at the time. When we can laugh, however wryly, we are tuning into the sparkle of the Spirit who is always there, hovering over the chaos.

Travel by public transport, as well as bringing its frustrations, is a community experience. If you use the same bus route regularly, you will probably recognize some of your fellow travellers and realize that you are part of a wider, inter-related society. But for many city-dwellers the commute to work on the bus or train has become a solitary matter, each passenger cocooned in a private world behind a newspaper or plugged into a mobile device. In the bustle of the city we can lead our whole lives in this self-isolating way. Is this how we want it to be?

FINDING THE WAY

Finding your way around is a major challenge of the journey. Whether you are navigating the one-way systems of your home town, or trying to work out where to go in an airport labyrinth, you will be looking for signs to guide you. This requires focus. If you allow every wrong turn to dismay you the journey will grind you down. Most of us make very many wrong turns in the journey of our lives. This was as true in Old Testament times as it is today. Let's join a band of travellers from the ancient world, as they set out on a journey into the unknown…

Led by Moses the children of Israel have been liberated from enslavement in Egypt and are on their way to the promised land. They think they know where they are going, but between the place of unfreedom and the place of promise there lies a journey that no one can predict or plan – a journey through the wilderness. The book of Exodus describes the convolutions of this journey, and we discover (in Exodus 13) some surprising details. These ancient asylum seekers are guided along their journey, even though that guidance is by no means always obvious. We learn, for example, that although there would appear to be a more direct road to Canaan, they are led by a convoluted route through the desert. But there is a reason. God knows they will have to overcome many difficulties along the way and will be tempted to turn back and give up on the journey. The complications of the route will make this impossible. We also learn that Moses takes a rather unusual piece of baggage with him – the bones of Joseph. Joseph was the traditional dreamer of dreams. To make a journey through the wilderness of life we will need to carry our dream, our vision, along with us, even though it may feel as though that dream is long dead and turned to dust. And then we hear that by day the travellers are guided by a pillar of cloud; by night, by a pillar of fire. Not the most reliable method of navigation, you might think, but in fact this guidance not only proves trustworthy, but it enables them to keep travelling both when they think they can see where they are going, and when they are in the dark, with no idea of how to proceed.

As we struggle through the traffic jams and diversions and road blocks in our lives it may be worth remembering that:

- what seem like unwanted twists and turns may teach us more wisely and guide us more soundly than our own idea of a more direct route;

- however lightly we travel, we must never let go of our deepest dreams;

- there is a presence and a conviction in our hearts that can be trusted to guide us, whether we think we can see the way or when we know we are lost.

In what personal ways does this ancient story speak to your experience?

TRUSTING THE ROAD

A story is told of a Canadian truck driver setting out in the middle of the night, to drive cross-continent from Montreal to Vancouver. He switched on the engine and the lights came on. He peered into the darkness and thought to himself: "I am setting out on a journey of thousands of miles and the lights only reveal a few yards of the road ahead. This is madness." So perhaps he switched off the engine, abandoned the journey and went home to bed. Or perhaps he started to drive. In which case he will have discovered that the light travelled with him.

It's hard to risk the first step into an unknown situation. It can help to remember other times in the past when we've felt lost and confused, and yet we set out in faith, and the way really did reveal itself if we just trusted the path.

Even harder to take on board is that our own little lives are a unique and essential thread in the weaving of a pattern for all humanity that we cannot yet discern.

I was once at a major London underground hub in the early hours of the morning, just as the first commuters were arriving, first a trickle, then a throng. I imagined each person who crossed that forecourt leaving behind a trail of coloured light, like a thread in a tapestry. At first the weaving was sparse, but gradually the tapestry took shape, each separate journey creating a thread in the total picture. Each of us leaves a unique trail as we journey through life but together these trails create a reality bigger than anything we can imagine. Your journey is a unique thread in that tapestry. It's your choice as to whether, today, that thread will bring a little bit more light or more shadow to the story of life for all creation.

REFLECTIONS ON THE JOURNEY

- Look back over your journey so far. Can you see how what appeared to be wrong turnings or unwanted diversions have nevertheless brought you to where you are today? Have you ever been tempted to give up on your spiritual journey? Did you go home, or did you keep travelling, and if so, did the light travel with you? What is the dream that keeps you going?

- Next time you travel on public transport, try to be more consciously aware of your fellow passengers. Set aside your newspaper or book. Disconnect from your technology. Simply be present to others in a mindful manner. They are also struggling with life's demands. Being quietly present to them can become a living prayer.

- Has a travel breakdown ever given you an opportunity to connect with, or even to help, another traveller, and perhaps turned a stranger into a friend? What about any breakdowns in the smooth running of your life, perhaps through accident or illness? What setbacks have you encountered, and how did you deal with them? Is there anything to learn from this past experience?

- Try looking back each evening over the journey of the day – the events, the people, the conversations, and the choices you made. How do you feel about it all? What are you proud of? What do you feel grateful for? Is there anything you regret and would want to do differently tomorrow? Connecting your outer and inner journey each day in this way brings life and love and wisdom to both of them.

"The price of anything is the amount of life you exchange for it."

Henry David Thoreau

THE
_M_ARKETPLACE

You might think the marketplace would be the last place you would expect to uncover the holy. Jesus famously drove the marketeers out of the temple and told them not to defile the house of God with their commercial transactions, because they were cheating people. What would he make of our marketplaces today – our shopping precincts and malls, our corner shops and specialist stores and even our ventures into internet shopping?

Just the act of going shopping reminds us of our mutual dependence on each other. Buying and selling help to make this interdependence workable. If God is in all things, then God is also in the many daily transactions we are involved in, inviting us to be discerning in our choices and to exercise integrity in our dealings. What does this mean for us in practice?

DEBIT AND CREDIT

I saw a fridge magnet once with the inscription: "When the going gets tough, the tough go shopping." It's easy to laugh away such a comment, but it does contain an uncomfortable grain of truth. There can indeed be a satisfaction in cruising the shopping mall and coming home with something new. Superficially it can be therapeutic and raise our spirits, at least temporarily. On the other hand, when the going *really* gets tough, there may well be no money with which to indulge this desire, or worse, we may be tempted to run up debt.

In fact "debt" is one of the big issues of the marketplace where the presence of the holy might cast a beam of understanding. The word "debt" used to mean something to be avoided. And then along came credit cards, and there was a subtle shift in our language. The word "debt" morphed into the word "credit", which has an altogether more acceptable, even desirable, ring to it.

If, as Christians believe, we see the divine expressed in the life of Jesus of Nazareth, we can reasonably ask ourselves how Jesus would respond to this change of vocabulary which has legitimized a level of debt that has become a deep and dangerous epidemic in our times. My guess is that he would not send us all on a guilt trip. He would have compassion for anyone caught in a debt trap. But he would surely have something to say to those who are profiting from other people's needs, especially when that profit has become so extortionate that even our elected leaders are concerned about it.

Financial misconduct has acquired a very high profile in our times. We can't do anything personally to root it out in high places, but we can, and must, look at our own dealings, and if we find ourselves wanting, ask for the grace to change.

GOLDEN CALVES AND SACRED COWS

However we finance our visits to the shopping arcades, there is another question hanging over our buying and selling. Everyone enjoys acquiring something new or beautiful or useful. There is nothing wrong with that at all. But acquisition can dominate our thinking, until we start to centre our lives around what is material and transitory, which – God knows – will never completely satisfy us. The book of Exodus (32:1–24) tells the story of the golden calf – a story warning us against "settling for less", when the divine is calling us to more than we can ask or imagine. Does the golden calf live today in the shopping malls, or on the internet trading sites? Let's join the children of Israel and see whether we notice any connections.

The children of Israel had become used to their holy leader, Moses, taking off to the mountains to commune with God, leaving them to fend for themselves down on the plain. One day they had had enough of this. Moses had been gone a long time, and they were impatient, and so they gathered round Aaron. "Moses has disappeared, off with his God, and who knows when, or whether, he will return to us. Make us a god we can see, whom we can make into our guide and model." So they began to gather all the gold they could find from the jewellery they were carrying. They melted it all down and forged it into the shape of a calf, and they made the golden calf into their leader and their god.

Moses returned to the people eventually, carrying the tablets of stone on which the commandments were inscribed, but he was so enraged by their faithlessness that he shattered the tablets, scattered the dust on the water, and made the people drink it.
(Adapted from Exodus 32:1–24)

It's not a pretty story. We can choose to see it as ancient history, nothing to do with us. Yet there are connections that we overlook at our peril.

We too get impatient when life doesn't seem to deliver its promise. We take our "gold", whether in cash or in "credit", and turn it into something

that, at least in the short term, *does* appear to deliver what we long for. We become so pre-occupied with this enterprise that we can easily lose sight of the deeper values that guide our lives – values such as love, friendship, loyalty, honesty and trust. We install our own versions of the golden calf in our lives and can all too readily become beguiled by them.

Golden calves can grow into sacred cows. What we think we want can become so important that it eclipses everything else in our lives. Legitimate need can develop into inordinate greed until family and community concerns are blanked out by the headlong pursuit of profit. Legitimate justice can become a culture of litigation, where every minor inconvenience demands compensation. The preservation of status and reputation, both individual and institutional, can silence the cries of the exploited and the abused.

There is a sequel to this story (in Exodus 34). Moses, we noticed, broke the commandments, quite literally, reflecting the way the people

had broken the spirit of the covenant they had enjoyed with God. But in the end mercy and compassion prevail. God provides a second edition of the commandments and invites the people to renew their covenant relationship with the divine. We too break the sacred relationship with the holy one by harming each other, and by settling for less when we are spiritual heirs to so much more. We too are invited, over and over, to go beyond the immediate satisfaction of all that is on offer in the marketplace, and to centre our hearts and minds not on the transient and superficial, but on the eternal treasures of love, compassion and integrity.

What might the holy one whisper to us as we go to market? Perhaps something like this?

When you sell, do so with integrity. When you buy, do so with discernment.

REFLECTIONS IN THE MARKETPLACE

The demands and the pressures of the marketplace challenge us to practise *discernment*. Discernment is about sifting all that life throws at us, and all that life tempts us with, and deciding wisely what matters more and what matters less, what is contributing to our own and the greater good, and what is tending to pull us down from the best we can be.

- Bring to mind three or four aspects of your life that you would say are the *most important* to you – those you would most dread to lose. Do any of them have any material or monetary value?

- Can you see any factors within yourself that are distracting you from what matters most in your life? What might tempt you to settle for less than that "most"? For example, is a desire to earn more money or have more influence distracting you from the family life you long for?

- What *external* pressures are tending to pull you off course – for example, the power of advertising, the blurring of the line between truth and deception in public life, the pressure to spend more than you can afford?

- What practices in our marketplaces and other business dealings do you think would provoke Jesus today into overturning the cash desks?

- In the light of these reflections, is there anything in your lifestyle or habits that you wish you could change? Can you bring this desire into prayer, letting it rest in the light of the holy?

Jesus warned us that "where your treasure is, there your heart will be". Where do you feel your treasure *really* lies?

"*Never doubt the power of a small group of committed people to change the world.*"

Margaret Mead

WINNERS AND LOSERS

In any town or city, the air will frequently be rent by the piercing sound of sirens, as emergency vehicles speed through the streets to reach people at the point of need. For some who hear it, the sound of a siren triggers prayer for those who have called for help. Sometimes these prayers are called arrow prayers, launched to the heavens on behalf of an unknown stranger experiencing an extreme situation. For all of us, the sound of the siren is a call, indeed a legal requirement, to clear the way and give priority to the ambulance, fire engine or police car on its way to attend an emergency.

PEOPLE FOR OTHERS

It is no accident that our reflection on the emergency services follows on from our exploration of the challenges of the marketplace. In general the marketplace is driven by the human propensity towards competition. This is the drive of the savannah, the drive for survival in a complex and sometimes ruthless environment. My product must be better than yours, otherwise no one will buy it. I must get better marks than you in the exams, otherwise I won't get a job. The relentless drive to have a bigger and better home or car or circle of influential friends than the next person can take over our lives.

Even small children in school are encouraged to be in competition with one another. The emergency services bring us face to face with the opposite tendency in human beings – the need and desire to be there for others where there is no payback, simply because that is the human thing to do.

As a community we make choices about how to use our collective resources. Most democratic nations that can afford to do so make a collective electoral choice to use public funds to enable all citizens to have free access to what they need when they are in trouble – medical care when they are sick, specialist skills when they need rescue, protection when they are exposed to criminal or other threats. As individuals we are also invited to make choices about how we will respond to the needs of others. These choices take us beyond competition, to co-operation; beyond exploitation, to caring; beyond selling, to sharing.

A story is told of a school catering for both able-bodied children and those challenged, either mentally or physically, in some way. Sports Day arrived, and the normal range of races were run, the winners being awarded their trophies. The parents duly applauded all the winners. Then came the race for the children who were variously challenged. The starter signal was given and they all set off along the track. All was going well, until one of the children fell. At that point all the other children in the race, with one accord, turned back to help their fallen friend. The child who had fallen was helped up again, all the children linked hands, and they ran the rest of the race together, crossing the finishing line hand in hand. And the onlookers gave them a standing ovation.

This simple and, I believe, true story teaches us something tremendously important: although at one level we applaud the "winners" in life, and encourage competition, when we see true altruism being lived out, we realize that we admire co-operation and compassion much more. The "losers" can reveal themselves as "winners" – winners of our hearts and minds, and winners of the challenge to reveal what it really means to be human.

There are many people in our society who live for altruism. These men and women have chosen to use their energies and skills in the service of those most in need. They include many people whose lives are unsung songs of heroism, rarely if ever acknowledged – those who sit with the sick and the dying, those who care for the elderly and infirm, those who staff the charity shops or man the lifeboat crews and mountain rescue teams, those who help the marginalized find their way through the welfare labyrinth or teach newly arrived immigrants our language so that they can function in society. All these people, and many others, are living from a source of compassion, and

not primarily from a desire for personal gain. Indeed, to our shame, we acknowledge that many such people offer their services unpaid, and many who are employed in the caring professions are very poorly recompensed, because they don't, and never can, make a profit.

WHAT MATTERS MOST?

Jesus tells an interesting and challenging story that could be loosely retold in the experience of our own times.

There was once a man who got on with his life in the normal way. He made a living as best he could, buying and selling, saving his profits, and accumulating his nest-egg, which enabled him to buy material things and to maintain a very comfortable lifestyle. He was proud of his property. It reminded him that he was one of the winners in the race of life. He was grateful to God for blessing him with a little bit more than his share of wealth. He even saw his material possessions as a sign of divine blessing. Until one day, as he was going about his business, he came upon a field, and heard that a great treasure – a pearl of great price – was buried in that field. He longed to find that priceless pearl, but land prices were exorbitant. There was only one way. He decided to sell everything he owned, and use the proceeds to purchase this field. When he had the field, he spent the rest of his life unearthing the great treasure that the field held. That pearl of great price became more important to him than all the other possessions in the world.
(Adapted from Matthew 13:44–46)

What is this treasure, this "pearl of great price", that is worth more to us than all the things we strive for and fight over in the marketplace? Perhaps those little children can give us a clue. When we truly look into our hearts and ask ourselves what really matters most, what really makes us human, we discover that the answer lies not in competition but in co-operation; not in profit but in service.

LIVING COMPASSION

Next time you hear a siren, remember all those in our society, whether they wear a uniform or not, who have chosen to live for compassion and service, and ask yourself:

- What do you value more – the glittering prizes gained in the competition of life, which only a few can win, or the muted, quiet beauty of the compassion revealed by those little children, which is available to all who have a heart for others?

- How can we best honour the work of those who spend their lives in the service of the greater good? Is there anything we can do, as individuals or in our society, to redress the balance between those who gain rich rewards by pursuing their own best interest, and those who earn a meagre living, or none at all, in lives of public service?

Jesus tells the story (in Matthew 18:10–14) of a man who had a hundred sheep, and one went missing. He left the ninety-nine in their safe pasture, and went off in search of the one that was lost, and in danger. What do you think Jesus might want to tell us about the debt we owe to those who on our streets today go after the ones who are lost or in distress, sparing nothing to bring them to safety? He reminds us that "your Father in heaven is not willing that any of these little ones should be lost". The same inspiration continues to drive every paramedic, every firefighter, every doctor, nurse, teacher or social worker, every prison visitor, every charity worker, and every good neighbour in our lives today.

The marketplace, of course, is not the enemy but the necessary partner of social services, which it helps to finance. It is simply a question of balance. How will you balance your own life energy in the scales where profit is weighed against compassion, loving care against personal gain?

"Peaceful living is about trusting those on whom we depend and caring for those who depend on us."

The Dalai Lama

GIVE AND TAKE

So many things in our daily lives, like going shopping, picking up a mail item, receiving a delivery or ordering something online, remind us of our mutual inter-dependence. If you stop to reflect on how you live just one day and what you need in order to do so, you will realize that everything depends on something or someone else. It is certain that almost nothing on your plate has arrived there without the efforts of others. Even if you grew the vegetables in your garden, you didn't make the tools that enabled you to dig the ground, or design the cooker that prepared them, or make the plates from which to eat them. Even if you made the jam, you didn't grow the sugar or make the glass jars or generate the power that cooked it. Whichever direction your thoughts take you, they will lead you beyond

yourself, and remind you how much you depend on others, and they on you, and all of us on natural resources way beyond us.

So all forms of distribution and exchange are essential functions in our inter-dependent human family. The sacred mystery in which all our inter-dependencies are held and sustained, is to be discovered in every link of this web of life. We discover the sacred in the post office, the delivery agencies, the public services such as refuse collection and disposal, the call centres and telephone exchanges. These are the visible agents of our constant need to be giving to and receiving from each other, whether money changes hands or not. They are also reminders of a constant call to gratitude.

ALL IS GIFT

The resources of the earth do not belong to us. Actually nothing belongs to us. That is hard to hear and almost impossible to acknowledge. A friar once gave a talk to a group of students about the life of a vowed monk. Afterwards one of the students asked him about the vow of poverty. "Poverty," he replied, "is simple. We don't have money." There was a slight intake of breath among the surprised students, at the apparent impossibility of such a situation. "We don't have money," he went on. "We only have the use of it." That sounds like an excellent arrangement, you might say – the use of money but not the responsibility for it. But what he was actually saying was something profoundly true. With or without vows, none of us actually owns *anything*; we only have the use of it.

A little child can show us how true this is. She wants to give you a present, but she possesses nothing, so she comes to you to ask for the bits and pieces she needs to make this present. Or an older child may simply ask you for the money to go out and buy you a gift. It's obvious that the child has nothing except what he has first been given by you. It's not so obvious that this situation continues as we grow up. You think you own your car? Your home? Your computer? How did you get it? You bought it

with the money you earned, you think. But how did you earn that money? You earned it by using your *gifts*. In the end, all is gift, whether it comes via the postman or via the gene pool. We all arrived on this earth with nothing, and we will leave it with nothing. Everything in between is pure gift. Ours to use, but not in any permanent way to own.

EUCHARIST – THE BIGGER STORY

To be recipients of all this gifting lays upon us two obligations:

- To give thanks for all we receive. This is not simply a matter of courtesy, but an essential attitude of heart that acknowledges our dependence on others, and ultimately on God, for all.

- To share and pass on what we have received. We can't hold on to anything and keep it to ourselves; we must be willing to share. Receiving obliges the recipient to keep giving. The resources of the earth must continue to flow, just as money must flow – hence the word "currency". As soon as we hoard too much away for ourselves, we obstruct this flow and somewhere along the line someone else will be deprived.

The word "eucharist" captures both these obligations in one symbolic act. It means "thanksgiving", and it also describes the Christian sacrament of sharing in the life of Jesus. The words we hear at a communion service, in various forms, express the command of Jesus to his friends at the last meal they shared after he had given thanks and broken the bread: "This bread, this wine, is my very self, given for you. Do the same for each other in remembrance of me."

Giving, distributing, receiving, giving thanks and then continuing to share. This is the dynamic that we celebrate in the eucharist. Let's pause for a moment on a grassy hillside in Galilee, where a large crowd has gathered to hear Jesus teach.

It had been a very long day. Jesus and his friends had, as they thought, escaped across the lake in a boat, to find some time and space to recover their energies, but, predictably, the crowd had followed them. Evening was closing in. They began to be concerned about how all these people were going to get something to eat. Jesus urged his friends to find a way to feed them all – an impossible task? The story tells that a small boy came forward and volunteered his own lunch pack to be shared – just five barley loaves and two fish. Hardly a feast for several thousand. But Jesus took the offering, gave thanks, and then asked his friends to distribute the bread and fish to the crowd. And everyone that evening had plenty to eat, and when they gathered up the scraps afterwards they collected twelve baskets of leftovers.

(Adapted from John 6:1–15)

This story really tells us all we need to remember about eucharist:

- The receiving of a meal that day depended on someone giving it – in this story, the small boy offers his own lunch.

- Before the meal is distributed, Jesus gives thanks.

- The food is then shared, passed from one person to another, until all are provided for.

Giving – receiving – thanksgiving – sharing. What is willingly and freely given multiplies in the giving. What is withheld and hoarded for ourselves shrinks and withers. There are countless ways of passing on this energy in obedience to Jesus' command: "Do the same for each other." Every time we give someone else an hour of our time, or the gift of a listening ear, or a simple act of kindness, we are passing on the energy of love, giving something of ourselves for them. This is a moment-by-moment way of *being* eucharist to each other.

LIFE AS EUCHARIST

Mindful of all those in our towns and cities who make possible, by their efforts, the receiving and distribution of all that we need for life, we can turn our response into a prayer of thanks, especially at the point of receiving something life-giving, such as a meal. Traditionally we call this "grace". One approach to this way of saying "thank you" might be a prayer of mindfulness:

- As you contemplate the food that is on your plate, say a silent "thank you" for all that has enabled it to be there: the sun and rain that energized and nourished its growth; the earth in which it grew; the people who grew it, gathered it, packed and delivered it, prepared and served it; any fish or animals whose lives were given that we might eat, and so on. This will remind you of the long chain of indebtedness we owe to so many other parts of creation whose energy has been spent to bring us this food.

- This food will now give *you* energy, as well as enjoyment and satisfaction.

- Now ask yourself: "All this energy has been spent to bring me this meal. How will I now spend the energy that this meal gives me, not just for my own satisfaction, but for the greater good of others, and of all creation?"

Giving – receiving – thanksgiving – sharing.

In this way the eucharistic cycle, which is a natural and sacred reality, not just an ecclesiastical rite, remains unbroken and continues to bless all it touches.

"*My humanity is bound up in yours, for we can only be human together.*"

Desmond Tutu

GATHERED
TOGETHER

Human beings only have meaning in relationship, so it has been wisely said. From the moment of conception we are in relationship with the mother who carries us, and the web of relationship widens with every new experience and encounter in our lives. Even the most naturally solitary among us have need of others. One of the worst punishments we can mete out to offenders is solitary confinement. Most of us, happily, won't experience this extreme of deprivation, but probably many of us can remember how it felt to be made to stand apart from siblings or classmates because of some misdemeanour or to be excluded by our peers from a game in the playground. To be separated from the peer group is a big deal, and instinctively we dread it.

A reflection of this need to gather together and form community is found in our high streets and town centres, in the many variants of gathering places we frequent: the pubs, coffee shops and restaurants, the social centres, the clubs catering for every kind of interest, and even at the school gates and in doctors' waiting rooms. In all these places we gather, we talk, we connect, we interact with each other. Gathering together is a crucially important part of what it means to be human. What does it mean to *you*? And are your favoured gathering places also sacred spaces?

THE GATHERED...

"*Where two or more are gathered,*" Jesus told us, "*I will be there among you.*" It is also true to say that wherever two or more are gathered, there will be a conversation. Relationship makes space for discovery, if we have the grace to listen with genuine interest to each other's stories, and the courage to share our own. If we can trust the promise that the sacred presence pervades our human gatherings, then that space of discovery also embraces the discovery of the divine in the ordinariness of a chat over coffee or an earnest discussion at the book group or a compassionate silence alongside a neighbour who has received bad news.

Many of our gatherings involve celebration of some kind, whether of a birthday, graduation or marriage, or of the life of someone who has now passed beyond our physical orbit, in a "wake". Jesus was no stranger to celebrations and he uses the example of a party to make a point one day. He has something to say to the other guests, and something to say to the host too. Let's listen in…

The guests, it seems, are concerned with taking the appropriate seat at table that reflects their rank and status. "Don't do that," he warns them. "Don't take the best seat. Imagine if someone more important than you arrives, and you have to move to a lower place. Think of the humiliation. Better by far to take the lowest place. If the host then invites you to move up the table you will be honoured, not humiliated. At the divine banquet, those with a high opinion of themselves will be humbled, but the modest will be honoured." Then he turns to the host: "When you throw a party, don't just invite your friends and family or those you think will repay your hospitality. Remember the poor, the disadvantaged, the lonely strangers, and embrace them in your circle of kindness. They can't repay you, but in the divine dispensation, love is its own reward." He then goes on to reinforce his point with a story: A prosperous man once prepared a great feast and invited everyone he knew. When the feast was ready, his servant went out to call the guests to table. But they all began

to make excuses. They were all too busy with other matters and sent their apologies. Eventually the host lost patience with his chosen guests, and sent the servant out again: "Go into the back streets, the slums and the homeless shelters and invite the destitute, the disadvantaged and the dropouts. Gather in the people who are roaming the streets with nowhere to go." And all came flocking to the feast, and there was plenty for all.
(Adapted from Luke 14:7–24)

How willing are we to participate in what is happening in our own communities? What excuses do we use when invited into deeper engagement with other people? I have several friends whose hospitality I frequently enjoy. I love them especially because I know what they themselves would probably not realize: that their table is often spread for people who can never return the invitation. I want to be more like them. It helps to remember that I'm not expected to invite *every*one to my table, but challenged to be willing to invite *any*one. An African saying declares that as soon as someone knocks on our door, he is no longer a stranger.

... AND THE EXCLUDED

But one person's gathering place can be another person's isolation. I could imagine a different version of the story that might go something like this:

Imagine that the same prosperous and kindly man had arranged a party, as in the first story. He had invited everyone in the neighbourhood, with no exceptions – rich and poor, young and old, worthy and unworthy – and had spared no expense in offering all comers the very best. A week before the day of the party, he was called away on business and left the final arrangements to his

servants, promising to return in time for the big day. But when he returned he found many empty places at the table. When he asked his servants why so many people had not come, they admitted, rather sheepishly, that they had made their own decisions about who was acceptable and who was not, and had sent some people away.

What do you think he would have said to the servants who had decided on these exclusions? What do you think he would have said to those who had found themselves excluded from the feast by the officious servants?

Do you find any connections in your own community with either of these stories?

Community has a shadow side. Its dark sibling is *marginalization*. Wherever human beings gather they tend to create divisions and exclusions. This applies as much to faith communities as to so-called secular gatherings, yet marginalization has no place in the model of love that Jesus embodies.

REFLECTIONS ON COMMUNITY

As you reflect on your own gathering places and your own community life, you might bring to mind some of these thoughts:

- What makes community for you? Where, and with whom, are your favourite gatherings? What is it that draws you together – perhaps a shared interest in some pursuit, or the fact of having

children at the same school, or the desire to go more deeply into particular interests such as music or literature or sport, or a shared passion for justice in some aspect of life, or a desire to volunteer your skills and service in a particular way? How do *you* enrich that gathering, and how does it enrich your life?

• How well do you know your neighbours? How many people in your street can you greet by name when you meet them? Do they have your phone number and are they really welcome to use it, if they need help?

• Are your wider community circles truly inclusive? Are the physically disadvantaged able to access the meeting places, for example? Are those with a different worldview really welcome to share your tea and biscuits, and your conversations?

• If you belong to a faith or church community, how does that community feel about people of other faiths, or of no explicit faith at all, or people with different ideas about social issues or religious expression? Is your faith community a tightly guarded nursery where only certain plants are welcome to grow, or is it a fertile field as broad as the earth itself, nourishing and being nourished by all – both friend and stranger?

• How might we make conscious choices that strengthen the bonds of community and work against any attitudes, in ourselves or in our groups, that are tending to leave others feeling excluded?

"*What we take in by contemplation, we pour out in love.*"

Meister Eckhart

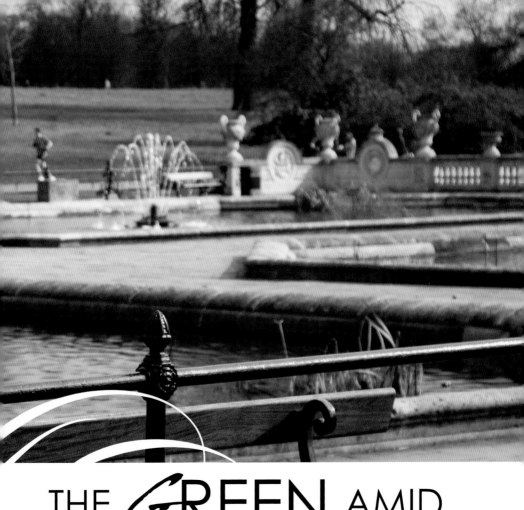

THE GREEN AMID
THE BROWN

Somewhere in every urban setting, or easily reached from it, is an oasis space that sings out loud the word "Life!" This might be a beautifully landscaped park, or a small green space in a city square. It might be a home-made window-box or a simple bird feeder hanging on a fence. It might be just the view of a distant tree from an apartment window, or the patterns of light and shadow, cloud and sunlight, that cross our skies, and our lives, each day.

LIVING WATER

Somewhere in the unrelenting cityscape is a spring of living water breaking out from a hard rock. This might be an elaborate water feature in a public place, or the duck pond in the local park, or a canal meandering through the industrial heartland, connecting the city to its rural hinterland. It might be as simple as a drinking fountain in the city centre or a baby's paddling pool in a neighbour's back yard.

These are oases that refresh our hearts and souls in the midst of the city's clamour. They make us feel more alive, and bring us a taste of a peace that is more than just the absence of conflict.

You might like to pause to reflect on where you find such oasis space in your neighbourhood and what it means to you. Where is the life-restoring green amid the urban brown? Where is the living water in the spiritually barren lands? To find the sacred presence in such places is to celebrate life and growth and the recurring pattern of dying back and renewal that the passing seasons reveal. It is to find that which leads to life in the sometimes harsh and unyielding situations that we face in our daily lives.

In 1845 the city of Dresden in the Saxony region of Germany was spared the ravages of the cholera epidemic that was sweeping the land. In thanksgiving, the so-called Cholera Fountain was constructed – elaborately sculpted and engraved with words from Psalm 91:5–7.

You need not fear the terrors of the night,
The arrow that flies in the daytime,
The plague that stalks in the dark,
The scourge that wreaks havoc in broad daylight.
Though a thousand fall at your side,
Ten thousand at your right hand,
You yourself will remain unscathed.

In 1945, exactly one hundred years later, Dresden was carpet-bombed by British and American aircraft. The historic city was almost totally destroyed and many thousands of people, including untold numbers of refugees, were killed in the firestorm that swept across the city, making the word "Dresden" an enduring symbol of the horrors of war. When the storm was over, almost nothing was left standing in the city, *except* the Cholera Fountain. If we re-read its inscription in the light of its history, what can we say about the terrors of the night and the scourge wreaking havoc by day? In spite of the terror it witnessed, and survived, the Cholera Fountain nevertheless speaks of life, and of something indestructible within the human spirit that cannot be quenched, whatever the circumstances arrayed against it.

To seek out the oasis spaces in our cities is to connect to this promise that there is a source of life within the human heart that will never cease to flow. This source assuages more than just our physical thirst. It addresses our deepest needs. It springs from the "God-shaped space" within us. The life-giving oases in our towns and cities are a very visible sign of this invisible source. They can help us to connect to it whenever we need it.

QUIET TRANSFORMATION

The kind of prayer that the oasis suggests is *contemplative*. We are simply present to the mystery, and though nothing seems to be happening – no eloquent words or profound insights – in fact a deep transformation is taking place. It reminds me of a story from the life of Jesus:

There was a wedding at a town called Cana in Galilee. Jesus and some of his friends, along with his mother, had been invited, and were, presumably, relaxing and enjoying the feast… until the word went out that the wine had run out. At first Jesus didn't react, but, prompted by his mother, he eventually intervened, and asked the servants to fill up six large empty containers with water. The servants did as he asked them. When all the containers had been filled Jesus asked one of the servants to draw out a cup and take it to the steward for tasting. The steward, who had no idea of what had happened, took one sip and declared it to be the very finest wine, unaccountably left to the end of the feast.
(Adapted from John 2:1–12)

This story has much to teach us, not just about Jesus but about prayer, especially contemplative prayer.

- It begins with emptiness. The containers were empty. We come to God in the emptiness of our hearts, helpless to help ourselves.

- In the silence and the stillness, a transformation begins. The emptiness is like that of a cocoon; it hangs on the tree apparently lifeless, but in fact it is a place of transformation as the butterfly takes shape within it.

- Through the flow of the Holy Spirit we are then filled to the brim in ways we cannot understand. Our emptiness provides space for the divine in-filling.

- We are then poured out, for each other and for the greater good, and only then does the transformation become apparent. If the wine is not poured out it might as well still be water. If we are not poured out we might as well still be our untransformed selves.

PRAYER AT THE OASIS

The oasis, whether physical or spiritual, is a source of refreshment, renewal and life. What aspects of your life are oasis spaces? How often do you visit them, either literally or in your prayer?

- Can you allow the sense of refreshment and renewal you experience in the green spaces of your town to awaken a parallel awareness of inner renewal in your heart?

- When everything falls apart, and your life seems to be in ruins, is there a "Cholera Fountain" anywhere? Perhaps it takes the form of a friend who is there for you, no matter what, or a faith that hangs on in there through the darkest hours. Can you be a fountain of life for others?

- Can you remember any times in your life when you have felt drained and emptied out, and yet, in hindsight, something poured in to fill that emptiness and transform it into something life-giving for yourself and for others? Sometimes life gouges out great holes in our hearts, but these can be the very places where new pools of healing gather.

- When the divine mystery touches our lives, and transforms them in some way, this is an invitation to us to allow ourselves to be poured out for others. When have you received the gift of an outpouring of loving-kindness from someone else? Can you allow yourself to be poured out too?

Take a gentle stroll through your town, and seek out the living water that is flowing in it, the green amid the brown. The oasis spaces in your town are also there in your heart.

"What lies behind us and what lies before us are tiny matters compared to what lies within us."

Ralph Waldo Emerson

FROM DAWN TO DUSK

I turn back my inner clock fifty years and revisit a scene that is for ever etched on my memory: a woman – grey-haired, with a slight stoop – strides purposefully through the school's spring gardens. She is our maths teacher. We live in dread of her sharp tongue, and yet know that any reproaches are always just. Soon she will come into our classroom and for a few precious minutes, before we enter battle with the calculus again, she will pause, her voice will soften, and she will tell us that the first snowdrops are just peeping through the still half-frozen ground in the spring garden. She will urge us to be sure to go and see them before their fragile season is over. Six months later we listen in stunned silence to the news that she has died, the best-loved teacher we ever had, a perfect fusion of strength and tenderness, her own fragile life now ended.

Wherever we live – town, city or rural idyll – we all encounter the drama of beginnings and endings throughout all our days, and the two can be very close neighbours. Sometimes new life bursts upon us unawares; sometimes it arrives gently, needing time to come to birth. Sometimes it is snatched away almost before it has begun. To walk the city streets at dawn or dusk can help us to connect not only to the drama of our beginnings and endings but also to the sacredness that enfolds them. It can help us to recognize the holy where we may feel it is conspicuously absent.

BEGINNINGS

While you were still asleep – or maybe not – the day began with a holy hour, as the birds welcomed the new day with their dawn chorus. An early walk through your neighbourhood will give you a free ticket to the concert. It has been said that a bird doesn't sing because it has a message. It sings because it has a song. Forget the "messages" that crowd your mind. Listen, for a sacred moment, to the song that your heart longs to sing. What is that song really about? Is anything preventing you from singing it?

As you are reading this page, a woman nearby, at home or in the local maternity hospital, is going into labour. A new life is beginning. Just to bring to mind this simple fact, this minute-by-minute miracle can be an invitation to ponder our own beginnings. What did we dream of becoming? Sometimes those early aspirations take shape in our later lives in ways we didn't expect, and might not even recognize.

ENDINGS

And just as surely, while you read, someone nearby, either at home or in hospital or a hospice, is taking their final breath. A life is passing away as another is beginning. A walk through the city streets as night is falling can bring home to us the fact of our own mortality. The bright lights can temporarily blind us to the shortness of our lives and offer us distraction and diversion, and yet inevitably the night falls. We find ourselves in darkness. The lights have gone out, but another kind of light reveals itself – the starlight and the moonlight – much greater, more lasting lights than the neon signs of cinema and night club. It turns out that life and death are not mortal enemies but equal partners in the infinite dance of life. Every ending is a new beginning but the future cannot come to birth in us until we are ready to cut the cord of whatever is holding us to the past.

AND THE ROAD BETWEEN

As I look back over my own years on earth I can see that no experience, no part of our story, is ever wasted. We may feel that we are living on stony ground, but many who have gone before us have discovered for themselves that this is the very place wherein the sacred mystery dwells. An ancient story (recounted in Genesis 28:10–16) tells us the same kind of truth:

A man called Jacob once made the journey to a place called Haran. Night fell while he was still on the road, so he settled for the night in a stony place. Taking one of the bigger stones for a pillow, he lay down to sleep in the place where he found himself, and as he slept, he had a dream. In his dream he saw a ladder that started exactly where he was lying and reached all the way up to heaven. As he watched, he saw angels going up and down the ladder, and he heard the voice of God saying: "I am giving you this land on which you are lying. The path that lies behind you may have been a story of obstacles and problems. What lies ahead is beyond anything you can imagine, but know only this: I am with you, whatever happens, going ahead of you, keeping you in my heart and guiding your steps. I will never forget you and I will fulfil everything I have promised you." Then Jacob woke, and looked around him, and said: "Truly, God is in this place, this stony ground, and I never knew it."
(Adapted from Genesis 28:10–16)

This story reminds me of a winegrower in the Cognac region of France, who planted a tiny vine sapling in the stony ground there. It grew, beneath clear blue skies, until it became a strong vine. Its strength came from the struggle it had to put down deep roots among the rocks. Its growth was also helped by the liberal piles of manure that were heaped onto it. Time passed, as time must always pass. The vine, bathed in the purest light, bore the finest grapes. The time for harvest arrived. The grapes were torn from their mother vine, crushed and fermented. The new wine was left again, and time passed, as time must always pass. And the day arrived when the fruit of the vine was found to have become not merely wine, but the finest cognac, which would bring life and warmth and inspiration to many.

Our lives are like that little sapling. They need the struggle life presents us with, and the clear light of divine and human loving. They need the manure that life throws at us, and above all they need time, to become all that they are born to be. Cherish the sapling. It is that of God within you, and within everyone you meet, however deeply buried. Engage with the struggle. Rejoice in the light. Welcome the manure for, believe it or not, it is nourishing your growth. Endure the crushing, and let time mature you into who you truly are.

REFLECTIONS FROM DAWN TO DUSK

- Take some time to stroll around your neighbourhood, noticing the young at play, or the growth of trees and flowers in park or garden. Where do you see new life coming to birth? Now look at your own life. It may seem like stony ground, but the struggle with the stones is making you stronger. Where do you see new life sprouting in your own life?

- Now visit your local burial ground. What feelings or memories does it evoke in you? Remember the losses in your life, especially any lost loved ones. Let your heart swell with gratitude for all they are to you, and don't be alarmed if that gratitude overflows into tears. Is there anything dying in your life right now? Anything coming to an end? Anything you need to let go of in order to discover the new beginning that it heralds?

- Try beginning each new day with a prayer of thanksgiving for the dawn and the return of light and life, and bringing to mind your plans for this new day, not forgetting that the best gifts of the day may well come as complete surprises.

- At nightfall, bring the day to an end with a simple prayer of reflection on all that the day has brought, giving thanks for the gifts, expressing any regrets you may have, and allowing the day to sink beyond the horizon of your consciousness as you entrust yourself to the darkness.

- Hear the promise of God (Jeremiah 31:13) to turn our mourning into gladness and make every ending a new beginning. When has this promise been fulfilled for you in the past? Can you trust it for the future?

"The day of my awakening was the day I saw, and knew I saw, all things in God and God in all things."

Mechtild of Magdeburg

EPILOGUE: *All Things New*

We have walked the city streets together, looking with fresh eyes at our own homes and workplaces.

We have strolled the markets and malls, observing people going about their business, or serving their fellow human beings for scant or no reward. We have revisited our favourite gathering places, and taken time out at the oases of stillness and calm in our frenetic city living. Has it made any difference to the way we see our ordinary lives? Have we uncovered some of the divine hiding places in the everyday?

The sacred is all around us, all the time. It is the reality in which we live and move and have our being. But it is our own lives that make this holiness incarnate, and make our places of living and working sacred, and therefore life-giving to all. The prophet Micah has a simple but powerful recipe for living our ordinary lives in the light of the divine within and around us:

What is good has been explained to you.
This is what Yahweh asks of you:

Only this, to act justly, to love tenderly
And to walk humbly with your God.
(Micah 6:8)

May there be justice in our dealings, integrity in our selling and discernment in our buying. May there be justice in our honouring of those who serve us and those whom we serve.

May there be love and tenderness in our homes, even when we don't feel loving, and whenever and wherever we gather together.

May there be mutual respect and wise leadership in our places of work, integrity in those who govern and those who are governed.

May we walk humbly, mindful that there is "that of God" within everyone we meet. May that humility guide all our dealings with each other – with those who have more, and those who have less than we do, those who agree with us and those who dispute with us, those who praise us and those who criticize us, those who help us and those who hinder us – and may we truly come to recognize the sacred presence in each and every one of them.

ACKNOWLEDGMENTS

This book is what it is because of the giftedness and dedication of four people in particular, to whom I would like to express my warmest gratitude. Thank you to Ronya Galka for her stunning photographic images of life in the city. Thank you to Ali Hull and Jessica Tinker for their sensitive editing and unfailing encouragement as the text took shape. And thank you to Jude May, who is responsible for the book's superb design.

All images (bar those specified) © 2015 Ronya Galka – www.ronyagalka.com
Page 46 image © i4lcocl2/Shutterstock.com
Pages 50–51 © xuanhuongho/Shutterstock.com
Pages 78–79 © Matthew Porter/iStockphoto.com

Published by Lion Books
an imprint of
Lion Hudson plc
Wilkinson House, Jordan Hill Road,
Oxford OX2 8DR, England
www.lionhudson.com/lion

ISBN 978 0 7459 5698 5

First edition 2015

Text Acknowledgments
Page 10: Scripture quotation taken from the Amplified® Bible, Copyright © 1954, 1958, 1962, 1965, 1987 by The Lockman Foundation. Used by permission.

Pages 12 and 92: Scripture quotation taken from The Jerusalem Bible, published and copyright 1966, 1967 and 1968 by Darton, Longman & Todd Ltd and Doubleday and Co. Inc, and used by permission of the publishers.

All other passages of scripture are the author's own translation.

A catalogue record for this book is available from the British Library

Printed and bound in China, February 2015, LH06